EXPLORE NORTH KOREA
12 KEY FACTS

by Molly Raben

12 STORY LIBRARY

www.12StoryLibrary.com

12-Story Library is an imprint of Bookstaves.

Photographs ©: Matej Hudovernik/iStockphoto, cover, 1; HelloRF Zcool/Shutterstock.com, 4; Richard Bradford/Shutterstock.com, 5; Uwe Brodrecht/CC2.0, 6; DickDaniels/CC3.0, 7; Alfo Co. Ltd./Alamy Stock Photo, 8; John Pavelka/CC 2.0, 8; William Proby/PD, 10; Astrelok/Shutterstock.com, 11; aphotostory/Shutterstock.com, 12; William Proby/PD, 13, 14; David Guttenfelder/CC4.0, 15; Luban/CC4.0, 16; ermaleksandr/PD, 17; Matej Hudovernik/Shutterstock.com, 18; NASA Earth Observatory, 19; William Proby/PD, 20, 21; Gilad Rom/CC3.0, 22; Uri Tours/CC2.0, 23; Roman Harak/CC2.0, 24; Kanokratnok/Shutterstock.com, 25; Mario Micklisch/CC2.0, 26; Uri Tours/CC2.0, 27; G7 Stock/Shutterstock.com, 28; Nannucci/iStockphoto, 29

ISBN
978-1-63235-559-1 (hardcover)
978-1-63235-614-7 (paperback)
978-1-63235-676-5 (ebook)

Library of Congress Control Number: 2018940819

Printed in the United States of America
Mankato, MN
June 2018

About the Cover

The Rungrado May Day Stadium in Pyongyang, North Korea is the largest stadium in the world. It has a capacity of 150,000.

12 STORY LIBRARY

Access free, up-to-date content on this topic plus a full digital version of this book. Scan the QR code on page 31 or use your school's login at 12StoryLibrary.com.

Table of Contents

North Korea Is on a Peninsula 4
North Korea Faces Environmental Challenges 6
A History Shaped by War 8
North Korea Is a Totalitarian State 10
The Economy Is Controlled by the Government 12
Students Must Learn about North Korea's Leaders 14
The Government Values Scientists and Engineers 16
The Infrastructure Needs Improvement 18
The Government Sorts People into Social Classes 20
The Arts and Culture Are Controlled 22
The Health Care System Has Problems 24
Daily Life in North Korea Is Challenging 26
North Korea at a Glance 28
Where in the World? 29
Glossary 30
For More Information 31
Index 32
About the Author 32

1

North Korea Is on a Peninsula

North Korea is part of the Korean Peninsula in East Asia. It is bordered on the north by China and Russia. On the south is South Korea. The Sea of Japan is to the east. The Yellow Sea is to the west. Many small islands are scattered along the western coastline. The total area of the country is 46,539 square miles (120,538 sq km). This is about the size of the US state of Pennsylvania.

Much of North Korea is covered by mountains, hills, and narrow valleys. There are wide plains along the western coast. Most of the farming takes place here. Along the eastern coast, narrow plains are backed by mountains.

The Nangnim Mountains run from north to south, through the center of the country. The Changbai Mountains in the north include North Korea's highest peak, Mount Paektu. It rises 9,022 feet (2,750 m). At its top is a large crater lake called Heaven Lake.

Rivers wind through the country's many valleys. The longest river is the Yalu. It flows 491 miles (790 km) from Mount Paektu to Korea Bay.

The Tumen River flows along the boundary of China, North Korea, and Russia.

Mount Paektu is sacred to the Korean people.

MOUNT PAEKTU'S BIG ERUPTION

In 946 CE, Mount Paektu exploded in one of the largest volcanic eruptions in human history. Rocks and ash were flung as far as Japan. Today the volcano sleeps, but not peacefully. Between 2002 and 2005, a number of earthquakes shook the giant volcano. Scientists monitor the mountain for signs of trouble. They worry that nuclear testing in North Korea might cause Paektu to erupt again.

7,722

Approximate square miles (20,000 sq km) of land available for farming.

- North Korea is bordered by water on two sides.
- Mountains, rivers, and valleys define the landscape.
- The country's farmland is along the western coast.

2 North Korea Faces Environmental Challenges

North Korea has four seasons. High temperatures during the summer months reach around 70 degrees Fahrenheit (20°C). Summer is a rainy monsoon season. Winter lasts from December to March. Temperatures in the south fall to around 20 degrees Fahrenheit (-7°C). In the north, they drop to -10 degrees Fahrenheit (-23°C). Snow falls mostly in the mountains.

The country has big environmental problems. They began in the 1950s, during the Korean War. North Korea and South Korea were fighting each other. The war caused many forest fires and much deforestation. In the 1990s, droughts and floods destroyed crops. Stored grain was washed away. Famine spread throughout the country. Starving people turned to the forests for firewood and food. More of the forest cover was destroyed. Deer, mountain antelope, goats, tigers, and leopards lost their homes. They

Limited resources for fertilizer lead to poor harvests.

The Eastern Curlew uses its long bill to fish out small shellfish from deep mud.

migrated to denser forests in the north.

The farmland in North Korea has been overused. The soil has few nutrients. Without trees and vegetation to hold the soil in place, erosion washes it away.

Birds can still be seen in the plains region. These include wild pigeons, herons, cranes, and many migratory waterfowl. The mud flats along the Yellow Sea have become a safe place for many birds. The endangered Eastern Curlew makes its home here.

North Korea knows it has environmental challenges. Because it is closed off from most of the world, it is hard to get help. Only rarely are foreign scientists allowed to visit. Some have reported that the country is experiencing an environmental collapse.

329
Approximate number of bird species in North Korea.

- North Korea has a rainy monsoon season.
- The environment has been damaged by deforestation.
- The farmland has been overused.
- There are many bird species in the plains.

3

A History Shaped by War

Korea was one country for centuries. In 1905, Japan invaded Korea. Koreans lived under Japanese rule until World War II ended in 1945. After Japan surrendered, the Soviet Union (USSR) and the United States split Korea in two.

The Soviet army occupied the north. US troops occupied the south. The plan was for the two parts to get back together one day. Instead, in 1948, the south formed its own anti-communist government. The north formed its own communist government. Its first leader was Kim Il Sung. Both sides claimed to be the true government of all Korea. When the south declared its independence in 1950, the north invaded.

This was the start of the Korean War. It lasted three years. The USSR and China helped North Korea. The United States helped South Korea. More than 3 million lives were lost.

Kim Jong Un crosses the DMZ to meet with South Korean President Moon Jae-in on April 27, 2018.

After the war, a demilitarized zone (DMZ) was built between the two countries. Both sides are heavily guarded.

Since the Korean War ended, the two countries have taken different paths. South Korea has a strong economy and a democratic government. North Korea is closed off from most of the world. It is known as the hermit kingdom. Its economy is underdeveloped. It has a large military and a nuclear weapons program. It has been ruled by the Kim family for more than 70 years.

2.5

Width in miles (4 km) of the DMZ.

- Korea was once one country.
- After World War II, the USSR and the United States divided Korea in two.
- North and South Korea fought each other in a war.

TIMELINE

1945: World War II ends. The USSR and the USA each occupy half of Korea.

1948: North Korea proclaims itself the Democratic People's Republic of Korea (DPRK).

1950: North Korea invades South Korea, sparking the Korean War.

1953: The United States and South Korea defeat North Korea. The DMZ is built.

1986: North Korea starts working on a nuclear reactor.

1994: Death of Kim Il Sung. Kim Jong Il becomes leader.

2006: North Korea conducts its first underground nuclear test.

2011: Death of Kim Jong Il. Kim Jong Un becomes leader.

2018: North Korea sends a team of athletes to the Winter Olympics in South Korea.

4

North Korea Is a Totalitarian State

North Korea is a totalitarian state under a dictatorship. The chief of state is the Supreme Leader of the country. Kim Jong Un has held this position since 2011. His father, Kim Jong Il, was Supreme Leader before him. Kim Il Sung, his grandfather, was the country's first chief of state.

Kim Il Sung started the Workers' Party of Korea (WPK). Led by Kim Jong Un, party members control all aspects of the government.

The Supreme People's Assembly is the legislative branch of the government. It has 687 members. They meet once or twice a year. Fifteen people from the Supreme People's Assembly are part of the Presidium. They handle the day-to-day lawmaking.

North Korea's military is called the Korean People's Army (KPA). It is

Kim Jong Un is known for his military-first policies.

part of the WPK. Kim Jong Un is Supreme Commander. All men and women are required to serve when they turn 17. The KPA has five branches. They are the Ground Force, Navy, Air Force, Strategic Rocket Forces, and Special Operation Force.

Roughly five percent of the population is on active duty.

NORTH KOREA AND JUCHE

In North Korea, Juche (joo-chay) is a set of political beliefs. The word juche translates to "self-reliance." Kim Il Sung came up with the idea. He wanted Korea to have political, economic, and military independence. This meant Korea should not work together with outside powers. It should not accept foreign aid. It should have a strong military to defend itself. Juche teaches that the Korean people can solve their own problems. But they must put their country and leaders first, before anything else.

1.2 million
Active members of the KPA.

- North Korea is a totalitarian state with a dictator, Kim Jong Un.
- The Supreme People's Assembly and Presidium make up the legislative branch.
- North Korea has one of the largest militaries in the world.

5

The Economy Is Controlled by the Government

North Korea has a centrally planned economy. The government makes the decisions. It controls the businesses that make the goods and services. Changes are slowly taking place. Today more people are selling their own goods and services. Markets are open where citizens can sell food and other products.

North Korea sells its resources to very few countries. Eighty-five percent of their exports go to China. Some of their main exports are coal, magnesite, iron ore, copper, and zinc. Other exports are limestone, lead, graphite, and precious metals.

Fishing is a big part of North Korea's economy. The country is between the Sea of Japan and the Yellow Sea. Pollack, sardines, squid, yellow corvina, and hairtail fish swim the waters.

Woven and knit fabrics are a large portion of North Korea's exports. Workers in North Korean factories make clothes that are sold all over the world.

North Korea has only a small amount of

Cargo ships use the Yalu River to reach the Yellow Sea.

THE POWER OF SANCTIONS

Many countries oppose North Korea's work on nuclear weapons. They try to stop the country from making these weapons. One way to do this is with sanctions. Sanctions are actions governments take against each other. Some block or ban certain kinds of trade. These can hurt a country's economy.

$1,343

Average annual income in North Korea.

- The government controls nearly all production of goods and services.
- Some people sell their own products at marketplaces.
- Mining, fishing, and textile production provide most of North Korea's exports.
- The country can't grow enough food to feed its citizens.

farmland. The country can't grow enough food to feed its own citizens. The government depends on other countries to help provide grain and other food. The people often face food shortages.

North Korea has 15 large garment export enterprises.

6 Students Must Learn about North Korea's Leaders

All schools in North Korea are run by the government. There are no private schools. Students are required to spend 12 years in school. Their education is free. After high school, students can attend university or vocational college. Examples of vocational colleges are factory college, fishing college, and communication school.

Classes in political ideology start in first grade. Children are taught about the Great Leader Kim Il Sung and the Great Guide Kim Jong Il. They study Kim Jong Un, the Supreme Commander, and Kim Jong Suk, his grandmother. Children learn they owe everything to the Kim family. They learn that South Korea, Japan, and the United States are their enemies. They are taught that South Korea started the Korean War.

Students also take classes in math and the

Portraits of Kim Il Sung and Kim Jong Il are in every classroom.

Red scarves symbolize membership in the Korean Children's Union.

natural sciences. Good jobs are available to those who do well in these subjects. Reading and writing are highly valued. Children study the Korean language, English, Russian, and Chinese characters. They learn about geography and history from the North Korean point of view.

All children join the Korean Children's Union. This is a political organization with ties to the Workers' Party of Korea (WPK), led by Kim Jong Un. It is for children ages 7–13. Each year, a big ceremony takes place at the Kim Il Sung Stadium in Pyongyang, North Korea's capital. Thousands of children are inducted into the Children's Union.

100

Percent of Koreans who are literate.

- The government runs the educational system in North Korea.
- Students are required to spend 12 years in school.
- More time is spent on lessons about Kim Il Sung and Kim Jong Il than any other subject.

THINK ABOUT IT

Do you think children should learn about their country's leaders in school? Why or why not? If you do, what should they learn about them?

7

The Government Values Scientists and Engineers

The North Korean government wants a strong nuclear program and powerful missiles. Scientists and engineers are needed for this work. They are given special privileges. They get the best apartments. They are given more food. People with degrees in science and engineering don't have to serve in the military.

In Pyongyang, the capital city, Kim Jong Un opened a street called Future Scientists Street. Scientists and engineers live there with their families. He opened a group of buildings shaped like an atom. People go there to learn about the country's achievements in nuclear science.

Scientists test the weapons they make. They learn from the tests how to make better weapons. In 2017, North Korean scientists tested 23 different missiles and one nuclear bomb. After

Future Scientists Street includes a school, sports park, and cellphone store.

Nuclear missiles are often paraded through the streets of Pyongyang.

successful tests, rallies are held to honor the scientists. They ride in motorcades past cheering crowds. Scientists are treated like national heroes. Parents want their children to become scientists.

Not all scientists work on weapons. Many study wind energy and solar power. Bioengineers look for ways to grow more nutritious food. Software engineers create new programs to help the economy. For example, design programs make it easier for clothing manufacturers to do their work.

$10,000

Monthly pay North Korea has offered scientists from the former Soviet Union.

- Some scientists in North Korea make and test nuclear weapons.
- These scientists are treated like national heroes.
- Other scientists study wind energy and solar power.

TECHNOLOGY FOR KIDS

Some scientists work at the Pyongyang University of Science and Technology (PUST). Scientists at its Center for Renewable Energy develop solar products. They came up with the PUSTCO Ray. This device charges in the sun. At night, it lights up. Children can use it to read without electricity.

8 The Infrastructure Needs Improvement

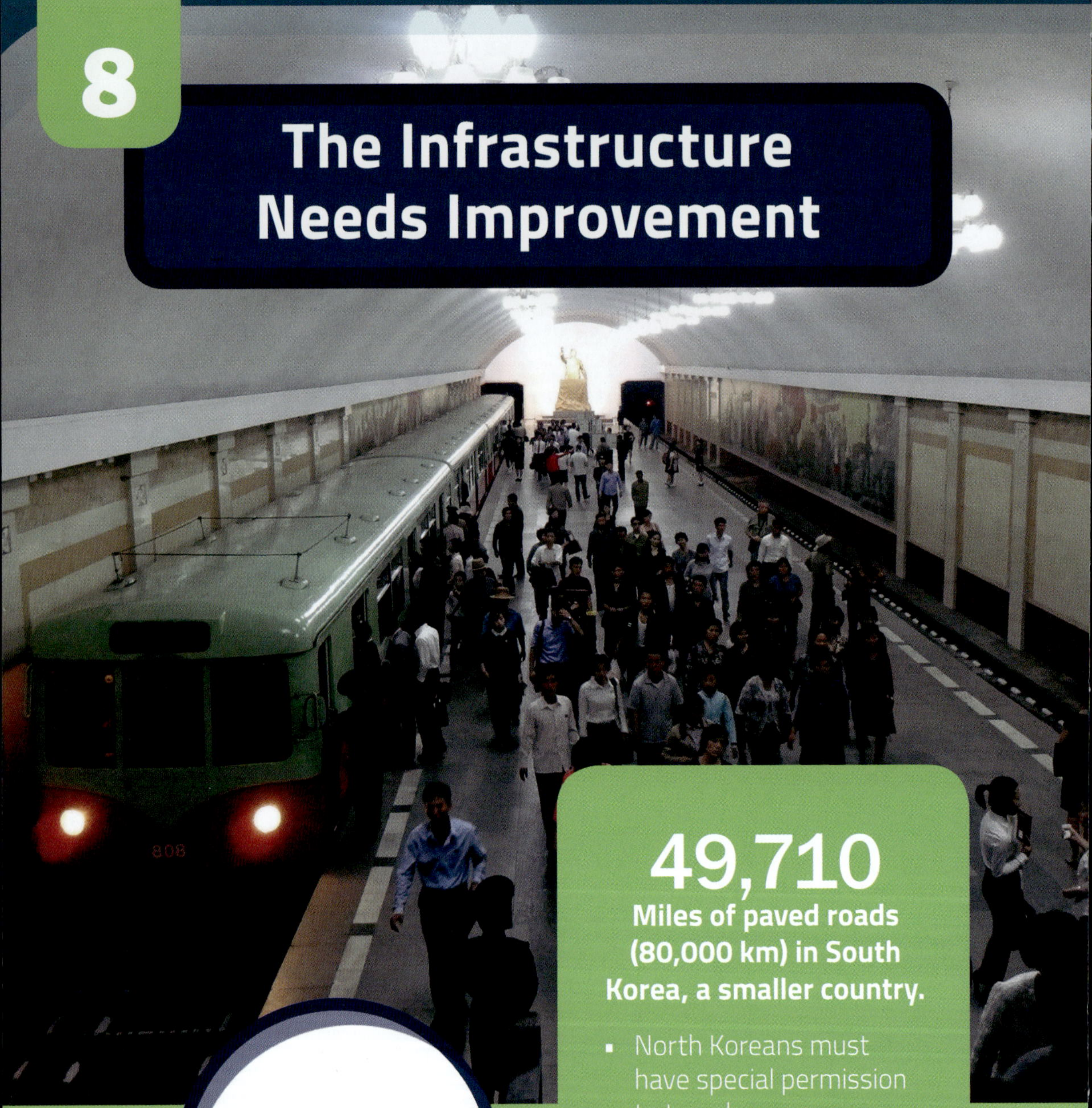

The train tunnels in Pyongyang double as bomb shelters.

49,710

Miles of paved roads (80,000 km) in South Korea, a smaller country.

- North Koreans must have special permission to travel.
- Railways are the most common means of transportation.
- Cars are mainly used by government officials and military personnel.
- North Korea is turning to solar power.

North Korea's infrastructure is outdated. People travel by old transportation systems. Electricity blackouts make daily life difficult.

North Koreans must have special permission from the government to travel around their country. Trains are the most common means of transportation. Most of the rail system was built before 1945. Some trains were updated in the 1960s and 1970s. A Trans-Korean Railway was built in 2000. It runs between North Korea and South Korea. People from North Korea rarely use this train. It is illegal to leave the country without government permission.

Cars have become more available to citizens in recent years. But they are mainly used by the government and the military. Outside of major cities, only 500 miles (805 km) of roads are paved.

North Koreans don't have enough electricity to power their lights at night. Satellite images show a country that is completely dark after sunset. Alternative energy solutions are helping to improve the electricity supply. Solar panels can be seen on nearly every apartment building in Pyongyang, the capital city. Hydropower supplies 60 percent of the country's electricity.

Cell phone use is on the rise. In 2011, the official cellular network Koryolink had 2 million subscribers. Mobile service was available in Pyongyang and 100 more cities. But subscriptions are expensive.

NASA satellite imagery shows how dark North Korea is at night.

9

The Government Sorts People into Social Classes

The core class makes up 28 percent of the population.

North Korea is home to more than 25 million people. Nearly 100 percent are Korean. The rest are people of Chinese descent. The country's official language is Korean.

People in North Korea don't choose their jobs or where they live. The government decides for them. Everyone is assigned a ranking called a *songbun*. A person's songbun is based on how loyal their families have been to the government. If they have done a lot for the government, they will have good songbun. If they have spoken out against the government, they will have bad songbun.

People with the best songbun are part of the core class. They can live in the capital city of Pyongyang. They can get good jobs working for the government. The next class is the wavering class. It includes average North Korean citizens. The lowest class is the hostile class. These citizens are most likely to work as farmers or miners. They live far away from any major city.

Members of the hostile class live in rural areas and do manual labor.

There is a special songbun category. It is called "awarded with an audience." It is for people who have talked to North Korea's leader for 20 minutes or had their picture taken with him.

CAN A SONGBUN BE CHANGED?

Recent changes have made it possible to move up in the songbun system. After working for three years, citizens can meet with members of their local government. If they have done good work and proved their loyalty, they might be granted a better songbun. If a person or a member of their family is charged with a crime, their songbun will drop.

17

Age when a North Korean citizen's songbun is determined.

- Nearly 100 percent of all North Korean citizens are Korean.
- The government decides where a person will work and live.
- A person's songbun is based on their family history.

10 The Arts and Culture Are Controlled

In North Korea, the arts and culture are used for political purposes. They are not forms of self-expression. They are controlled by the state and the Workers' Party of Korea (WPK).

Writers and artists can only make work about the government and its leaders. Large statues of Kim Il Sung, Kim Jong Il, and Kim Jong Un are seen everywhere. Musicians, dancers, and actors perform in organizations run by the government. These include the National Theater for the Arts and the State Symphony Orchestra.

The Moranbong Band is a popular music group. It performs songs about Kim Jong Un. Songs in North Korea have titles like "Long Life and Good Health to the Leader."

Newspapers are censored. Radios receive only North Korean broadcasts. Legal TVs are tuned to state-controlled programming. In 2016, Kim Jong Un started a video streaming service. Most of the programs are about North Korea's government and leaders. Many citizens have a TV and DVD player. Movies from other countries are

A mural of Kim Il Sung addressing the North Korean people stands in Pyongyang.

THINK ABOUT IT

Who are some musicians you enjoy listening to? What are their songs about? What topics do they address?

forbidden. But people find ways to buy and watch foreign films.

North Koreans celebrate national holidays that commemorate events in their history. The Day of the Sun on April 15 is the most important holiday. It celebrates the birth of Kim Il Sung, North Korea's first Supreme Leader. Grand military parades take place on this day. Thousands of people join the festivities in Pyongyang.

17

Number of national holidays in North Korea.

- All forms of art in North Korea praise the government and its leaders.
- Many North Koreans enjoy watching movies and TV.
- Some people watch films from other countries, even though they are forbidden.
- North Korea's most important holiday celebrates the birth of Kim Il Sung.

Thousands of North Koreans come out to cheer at military parades.

11 The Health Care System Has Problems

Health care is free for all citizens in North Korea. Mass vaccination programs help prevent disease. State hospitals provide medical services to those in need. But hospitals struggle to care for their patients. Equipment is old or broken. Broken equipment isn't repaired because parts aren't available. Medical supplies are scarce. Electricity blackouts are common.

Doctors are paid by the government, so their wages are low. Some doctors allow patients to visit their homes. People pay to do this. They know they will get better medical care. People also pay for their own medicine. Some pay a high price for Chinese medicines that are smuggled in.

Malnutrition is a frequent problem. People who lived through the famine in the 1990s did not have enough food to grow. Young men in North Korea tend to be one to three inches shorter (3–8 cm) than young men in South Korea. Malnutrition also affects the immune system. Because North Koreans often face food shortages, they are more likely to get sick or catch diseases.

All hospital equipment provided by the Supreme Leader is marked with a red label.

North Koreans are shorter than South Koreans, probably due to food shortages.

Cardiovascular disease is a leading cause of death. Many North Koreans have tuberculosis, malaria, and hepatitis B. More than half of all adult males smoke cigarettes.

THINK ABOUT IT

What diseases affect people where you live? Which ones are related to poor nutrition? Read and research online to find answers.

70

Average life expectancy in years of North Korean people today.

- North Korean citizens have free health care.
- Hospitals have a hard time caring for patients.
- Many North Koreans choose to pay a doctor for better care.
- Cardiovascular disease and malnutrition affect many citizens.

12

Daily Life in North Korea Is Challenging

Daily life for average citizens in North Korea can be very difficult. People work for long periods of time without a day off. They may earn only a few dollars a month. Some never get enough to eat. Many North Koreans sell goods and services on their own. Some bring in illegal goods, like films from China and South Korea.

North Koreans live under strict surveillance. Since 2010, the government has bought tens of thousands of closed-circuit cameras from China. Phone calls are monitored. People who try to communicate with the outside world are sent to prison camps.

North Koreans enjoy spending time with family and friends.

The entrance fee for the Munso Water Park is too expensive for most citizens.

Citizens spy on each other. They are encouraged to report anything that seems suspicious.

Still, North Koreans find ways to enjoy themselves. They spend time with family and friends. They go to movies and house parties. Karaoke is a favorite activity for those who can afford it. Amusement parks are a way to escape daily life. North Koreans love to stroll, but not at night. The streets are completely dark then.

People in North Korea also love to play sports. Basketball, soccer, and volleyball are among their favorite games. Taekwondo is popular.

37

Size in acres (15 hectares) of Munsu Water Park in Pyongyang.

- Some people in North Korea earn money by selling illegal goods.
- Citizens are under strict surveillance by the government.
- Amusement parks are an escape from daily life.

THE INTERNET IN THE HERMIT NATION

Most citizens in North Korea can't access the internet. For those who can, only a few sites are available. Most of these focus on the daily activities of Kim Jong Un. Internet rooms have been set up in elite universities. But when students use the internet, someone else watches them.

North Korea at a Glance

Population in 2018: 25,610,672

Area: 46,539 square miles (120,538 sq km)

Capital: Pyongyang

Largest Cities: Pyongyang, Hamhung, Namp'o, Hungnam

Flag:

National Language: Korean

Currency: North Korean Won

What people who live in North Korea are called: North Koreans

Where in the World?

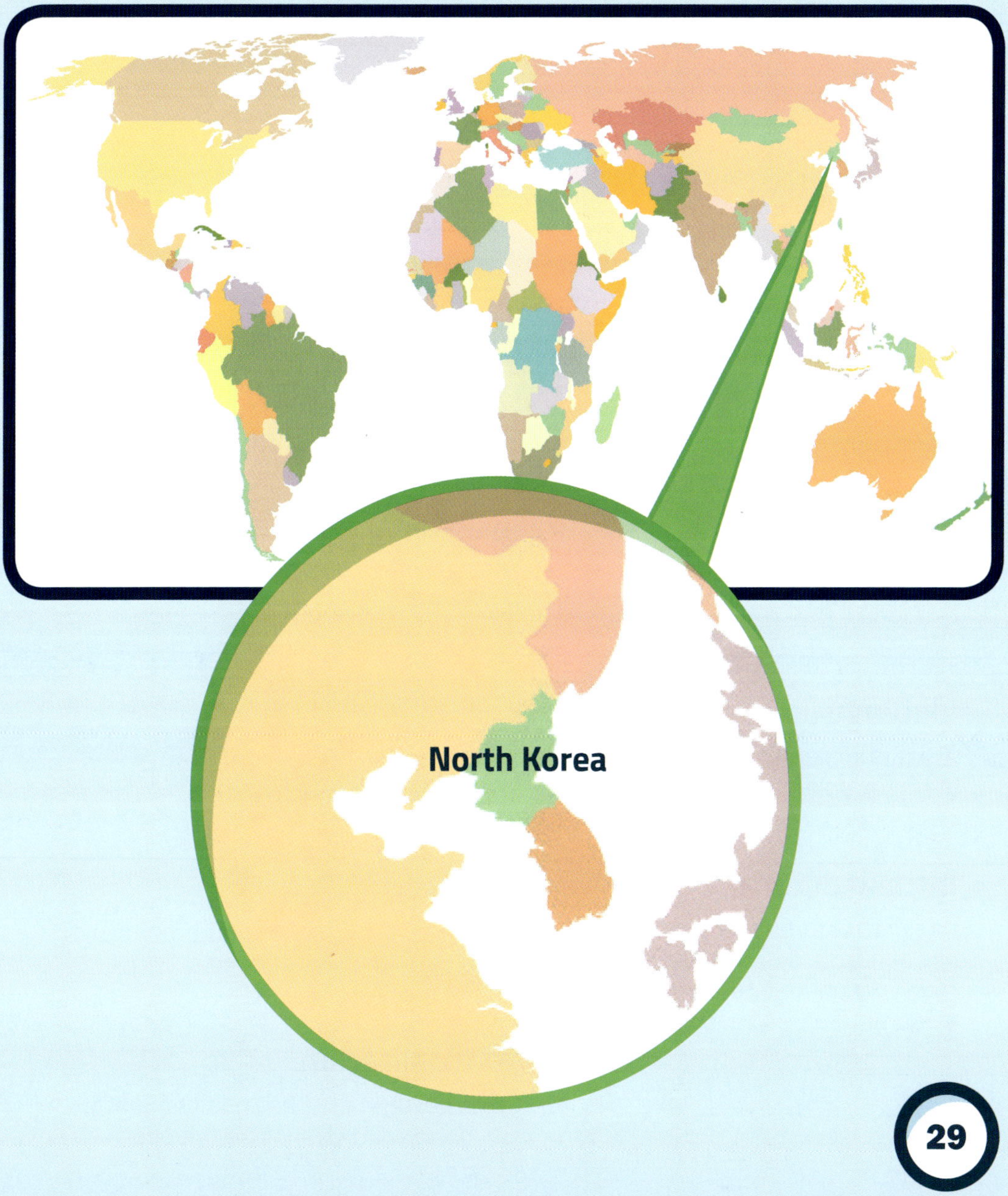

Glossary

communist government
A government controlled by a single political party.

deforestation
When trees are removed or cleared from a forest.

dictator
A ruler with complete power over a country.

famine
An extreme shortage of food, often caused by natural disasters or war.

ideology
A set of beliefs or ideas shared by a group or political party.

infrastructure
Basic structures and systems needed for a country to function, like roads, bridges, and communication systems.

literacy
The ability to read and write.

malnutrition
A condition caused by not getting enough to eat or not eating enough healthy foods.

peninsula
Land surrounded by water on three sides.

propaganda
Information used to promote or publicize a political cause.

sanction
An action taken to force a country to obey international laws. Examples are limiting trade or cutting off economic aid.

surveillance
Close observation of the behaviors and activities of citizens.

totalitarian
A government that has complete power and cannot be opposed.

For More Information

Books

Murray, Julie. *North Korea*. Minneapolis, MN: Abdo Publishing, 2016.

Raum, Elizabeth. *North Korea.* Countries Around the World. Mankato, MN: Heinemann-Raintree, 2012.

Visit 12StoryLibrary.com

Scan the code or use your school's login at **12StoryLibrary.com** for recent updates about this topic and a full digital version of this book. Enjoy free access to:

- **Digital ebook**
- **Breaking news updates**
- **Live content feeds**
- **Videos, interactive maps, and graphics**
- **Additional web resources**

Note to educators: Visit 12StoryLibrary.com/register to sign up for free premium website access. Enjoy live content plus a full digital version of every 12-Story Library book you own for every student at your school.

Index

bird species, 7

China, 4, 8, 12, 26
communist government, 8, 30

deforestation, 6-7, 30
demilitarized zone (DMZ), 8-9

economy, 9, 12-13, 17
exports, 12-13

farmland, 5, 7, 13
fishing, 12-13, 14
food shortage, 13, 24, 30

holidays, 23
hydropower, 19

Japan, 4-5, 8, 12, 14
Juche, 11

Kim Il Sung, 8-9, 10-11, 14-15, 22-23
Kim Jong Il, 9, 10, 14-15, 22
Kim Jong Un, 9, 10-11, 14-15, 16, 22, 27
Korean War, 6, 8-9, 14

malnutrition, 24-25, 30
military, 9, 10-11, 16, 18-19, 23
mining, 13
missiles, 16-17
monsoon season, 6
Mount Paektu, 4-5

Pyongyang, 15, 16-17, 18-19, 20, 22-23, 27, 28

solar power, 17, 18
songbun, 20-21
South Korea, 4, 6, 8-9, 14, 18-19, 24, 26
Soviet Union, 8, 17
sports, 16, 27

transportation, 18-19
Tumen River, 4

United States, 8-9, 14

volcano, 5

Yalu River, 4, 12

About the Author

Molly Raben is a children's author and musician from Minneapolis, Minnesota. She enjoys reading and researching about places she's never been. When she is not reading, writing, or playing music, she enjoys going on hikes with her rescue dog, Joni.